FAITH EXPERIENCES

taking time together

FOR TEENS AND PARENTS

FAITH EXPERIENCES

taking time together

FOR TEENS AND PARENTS

Joanne Loecher, OSF

Saint Mary's Press
Christian Brothers Publications
Winona, Minnesota

I wish to acknowledge and thank the following people for their contributions to the making of this book: to Barb Bunkers, for "Thanks for the Memories"; Jan Munz, for "Signed, Sealed, Delivered, I'm Yours" and overall collaboration; and Judy Tibor, for typing and computer programming.

Also thanks to the many parish directors of religious education, catechists, parents, and students in the Diocese of Winona who gave feedback and support.

Genuine recycled paper with 10% post-consumer waste.
Printed with soy-based ink.

The publishing team for this book included Robert P. Stamschror, development editor; Rebecca Fairbank, manuscript editor; Gary J. Boisvert, typesetter; Maurine Twait, art director; Rick Korab, Punch Design, cover designer; candle photograph by Tom Wright; pre-press, printing, and binding by the graphics division of Saint Mary's Press.

All clip art is from *Cartoon Clip-Art for Youth Leaders,* by Ron Wheeler (Grand Rapids, MI: Baker Book House Company, 1987). Copyright © 1987 by Baker Book House Company. Used with permission.

The photos in this book are from several parishes in the Diocese of Winona.

The scriptural quote on page 24 is from the New Revised Standard Version of the Bible. Copyright © 1989 by the Division of Christian Education of the National Council of the Churches of Christ in the United States of America. All rights reserved.

Printed in the United States of America

Printing: 9 8 7 6 5 4 3 2 1

Year: 2004 03 02 01 00 99 98 97 96

ISBN 0-88489-386-3

TABLE OF
contents

introduction   *7*

Handout A: Parent Evaluation   *12*

Handout B: Teen Evaluation   *13*

Handout C: Prayer Service: Giving Thanks for Family   *14*

EXPERIENCE 1

getting to know you   *15*

Handout 1–A: Special Features of the Experiences   *19*

EXPERIENCE 2

say what?   *20*

Resource 2–A: Directions: Say What?   *22*

Handout 2–A: Is It a Sin?   *23*

Resource 2–B: Sin Is . . .   *24*

Resource 2–C: God Says, I Say   *25*

Handout 2–B: Cartoon Characters   *26*

EXPERIENCE 3

thanks for the memories   *30*

Resource 3–A: Directions: Thanks for the Memories   *32*

Handout 3–A: Our Family Tree   *33*

Handout 3–B: Memory Cards   *34*

EXPERIENCE 4

highway to heaven   *35*

Resource 4–A: Game Board: Highway to Heaven   *28*

Resource 4–B: Card Set 1   *37*

Resource 4–C: Card Set 2   *39*

Resource 4–D: Card Set 3   *41*

Resource 4–E: Directions: Highway to Heaven   *43*

EXPERIENCE 5

signed, sealed, delivered   *44*

Resource 5–A: Signed, Sealed, Delivered, I'm Yours   *47*

Resource 5–B: Descriptions of Crosses   *48*

Handout 5–A: Sealed   *49*

EXPERIENCE 6

what's it to ya?   *50*

Resource 6–A: Sample Collage   *52*

Resource 6–B: Directions: What's It to Ya?   *53*

Resource 6–C: Value Cards   *54*

introduction

background and history

Strong communication between teens and parents helps foster faith formation in young people. After becoming convinced of this reality, a group of parish directors of religious education and catechists in the Diocese of Winona brainstormed and discussed ways to facilitate this communication. *Taking Time Together* emerged as a creative and effective way to enable this communication and enhance faith formation in young people and their families.

The activities in this book have been used successfully in many parishes, both rural and urban, within the Diocese of Winona. The activities are positive, enriching, and fun for both teens and parents. Once parishes have experienced them, they often follow up by creating additional activities of their own based on this model.

audience

Taking Time Together is intended for use with junior high students (grades 7–9) and their parents, guardians, or significant adults. (Hereafter the term *parents* is meant to include parents, guardians, and other significant adults.) But the activities have also been used successfully with tenth graders and their parent(s). The activities work well with groups of five to sixty participants.

purpose

In contemporary U.S. culture, daily life is often lived in the "fast lane." The time demands on families can be overwhelming. Without a deliberate effort to plan quality family time, communication—including communication about faith and religion—between parents and children can dissolve and relationships can weaken. The purpose of the faith-sharing experiences in this book is to provide the time and the opportunity for teens and parents to get together in a comfortable setting to reflect on and discuss a variety of faith themes and issues.

program design

The program consists of six faith experiences. The first one is an orientation and community-building experience for the whole group. The other five are designed for one-on-one communication between teens and their parents.

suitable situations and settings

These faith-sharing experiences are best used together in a single event that complements current parish faith formation programs for young people, such as parish religious education classes, youth ministry gatherings, re-treats, confirmation preparation, and the like. The event can be scheduled during the school year or summer, either on a weekday evening or on a weekend. Before or after the parish Sunday liturgy may be an ideal time for the get-together.

The best physical setting for the experiences is a large room such as a gymnasium, cafeteria, or parish center. A substantial area provides sufficient space for the opening icebreakers, prayers, and the individual tables needed for each activity. A sense of community happens best when all the activities take place in one large space, with the whole group experiencing them at the same time.

However, if a large room is not available, you can adapt the experience to whatever facility you might have. For example, one room can be used for icebreakers and prayer, while another room can be designated for the faith-sharing experiences. The faith-sharing experiences could even be set up in separate rooms if necessary.

the role of the facilitator

Someone needs to assume overall responsibility for the program. That person is called the facilitator. Although volunteers can be recruited to assist with details and specific tasks, it is crucial to have a facilitator who is familiar with the vision and the purpose of the program.

The following is a checklist of tasks that need to be done to facilitate the experiences:

before the experience
- ○ Determine costs and prepare a budget.
- ○ Get permission and support from the pastor or parish administrator.
- ○ Reserve the facility.
- ○ Mark the event on the parish calendar.
- ○ Provide for publicity, for example, posters in the vestibule of the church, notices in the parish bulletin, or fliers.
- ○ Designate a prayer leader.
- ○ Recruit and train any volunteer helpers that you may need.
- ○ Obtain all necessary supplies for each faith experience.
- ○ Prepare all the materials required for each faith experience.
- ○ Have refreshments available.
- ○ Check the meeting space for neatness. Make sure to set up the correct number of tables and chairs.
- ○ Be sure that the temperature in the meeting space is comfortable and that there is proper ventilation.
- ○ Set up a speaker's stand and a microphone, if needed.

during the experience
- ○ Greet the participants individually as they arrive.
- ○ Welcome the participants as a group once all have assembled.
- ○ Assure the participants that all necessary directions are located at the individual activity centers.
- ○ Make closing remarks.

after the experience

○ Collect evaluations, tabulate them, and share them with the pastor or parish administrator and the parish director of religious education.

○ Return everything in the meeting space to its original order.

○ Thank all who assisted and make plans for the next faith-sharing event.

The "materials needed" list and "preparation and setup" section for each experience will be of immense help to the facilitator and others working with the program.

overview

The faith-sharing experiences begin with a whole-group gathering, featuring two icebreakers followed by a prayer. After the whole-group event, the participants separate into family groups. Each experience is set up on a separate table, or tables if more than one setting is needed for each experience. Tables of like experience should be grouped together. The family groups move from table to table, participating in each of the five faith-sharing experiences.

After the families complete all the experiences, they go to a table containing evaluation sheets—one for the parents and one for the teens—and evaluate the experience. Handout A, "Parent Evaluation," and handout B, "Teen Evaluation," can be found at the end of this introduction. Depending on time constraints, families may need to depart after the evaluation. However, for those who can stay, it is best to conclude the time together with a prayer service and refreshments. A concluding prayer service is provided on handout C, "Prayer Service: Giving Thanks for Family," located at the end of this introduction. Invite six volunteers to help with the readings for the prayer service.

As previously noted, each faith experience requires a separate setting. Card tables work well. If long cafeteria tables are used, the ends of the tables can be used to accommodate separate settings. Four of the activities are designed to be experienced by each family alone. Three chairs are needed at these settings. One activity ("highway to heaven") is experienced by two families together. Six chairs are needed at this setting. Of course, you may need to adjust the number of chairs if some families have more than one child attending.

The time frame for completing all the activities is approximately 90 minutes. However, some of the activities take longer than others. You need to have enough settings available for each activity so that families can experience them without having to wait. (A grid is provided on the next page to help you determine the number of settings you will need to accommodate the number of families present.)

At this point you may feel a bit overwhelmed by the preparation that seems necessary. But remember that once you have prepared the materials initially, you will be able to use them again and again. Believe me, the effort is worthwhile.

The following items will need to be set up before the families arrive:

○ a name tag for each person
○ a table with markers to sign in and fill out name tags
○ a pencil or pen for each person, placed on the evaluation table
○ refreshments
○ copies of handout A, "Parent Evaluation," and handout B, "Teen Evaluation," placed on the evaluation table
○ a box for collecting completed evaluations

Upon arrival, all the participants should gather in the meeting space. Waiting to start until most parents and teens have arrived is best, but do try to start on time.

estimating the number of settings needed

experience	number of families				
	10	**20**	**30**	**40**	**50**
say what?	2 sets	4 sets	6 sets	8 sets	10 sets
thanks for the memories	2 sets	4 sets	6 sets	8 sets	10 sets
highway to heaven	2 sets	4 sets	6 sets	7 sets	8 sets
signed, sealed, delivered: part A	1 set	2 sets	2 sets	3 sets	3 sets
part B	3 sets	6 sets	8 sets	10 sets	12 sets
what's it to ya?	2 sets	4 sets	5 sets	7 sets	8 sets

Parent Evaluation

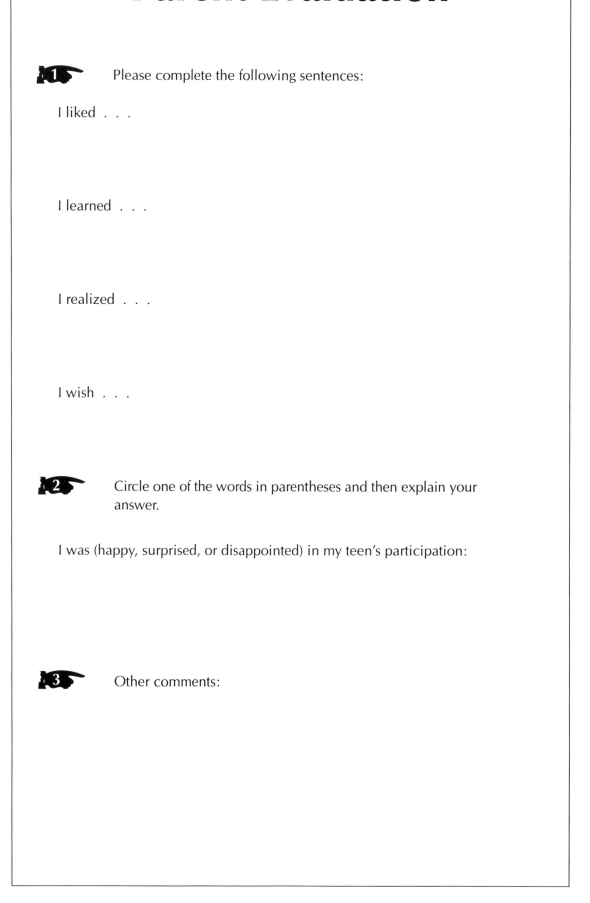

1   Please complete the following sentences:

I liked . . .

I learned . . .

I realized . . .

I wish . . .

2   Circle one of the words in parentheses and then explain your answer.

I was (happy, surprised, or disappointed) in my teen's participation:

3   Other comments:

     Handout A: Permission to reproduce this handout for program use is granted.

Teen Evaluation

1. Please complete the following sentences:

I liked . . .

I learned . . .

I realized . . .

I wish . . .

2. Circle one of the words in parentheses and then explain your answer.

I was (happy, surprised, or disappointed) in my parent's participation:

3. Other comments:

Prayer Service: Giving Thanks for Family

Leader: As we turn our eyes to the Christ candle, we express gratitude for this holy time together. Let us pause for a moment of silent prayer. [Pause.]

We are grateful, Lord Jesus, for your light that leads us in the way you have taught. You have called us to walk together with trust in you and in one another. Help us always to remember that your Spirit strengthens us to bring the light of hope and peace to others.

Prayers of Thanksgiving for Each Experience

Reader 1: Lord, you have blessed us with your love, which comes through family and community. May we respect and help one another, remembering your example of care.

All: We praise you for the gift of family and community.

Reader 2: Lord, you invite us to walk in friendship with you. Sometimes we fail and choose evil over good. Your forgiveness strengthens us to put sin behind us and go forward in your love.

All: We praise you for the gift of forgiveness.

Reader 3: Lord, wonderful memories of your presence fill our hearts. Help us to cherish the people who have been signs of your love.

All: We praise you for the gift of memory.

Reader 4: Lord, we are on a journey to everlasting life with you. Thank you for giving us faith to live our baptismal commitment to you.

All: We praise you for the gift of faith.

Reader 5: Lord, sometimes our journey is difficult. Your love for us, even unto death, offers us hope and encouragement.

All: We praise you for the gift of your life, death, and Resurrection.

Reader 6: Lord, many values fill our lives. As we make choices each day, may we call forth your Spirit of wisdom.

All: We praise you for the gift of your Spirit.

Leader: Now let us extend a sign of Christ's peace to one another and go forth strengthened by the Spirit of Jesus.

EXPERIENCE
1

getting to know you

focus

Experience 1 is unique because it is the only one of the six experiences in which all the families participate as one group. The experience is intended to create an atmosphere of welcome, openness, and trust among the participants. Faith sharing thrives in such an atmosphere and is deepened through prayer.

materials needed

○ a bell, whistle, or other noisemaker
○ a paschal candle displayed on a tall stand
○ a pillar candle in a candle holder for every four or five families
○ matches
○ a tape or CD player
○ a tape or CD of reflective background music, such as "Reflections," by the Dameans (Damean Music, Phoenix, AZ), or "Reflections," by Adam Martin Geiger (LuraMedia, San Diego)
○ a copy of handout 1–A, "Special Features of the Experiences," for each family

facilitating the experience

welcome

Welcome the participants in the following, or similar, words:

> It's great to see all of you! It is especially wonderful to see families together!
>
> Jesus once said something to the effect: "If you want to know my Father, get to know me. And if you want to know me, look within your own heart and into the faces of one another. You will discover my presence there" (John 14:7).
>
> That is what we are here to do: to get to know ourselves, one another, and our God just a little bit better. We will come to know God through our understanding of Jesus and ourselves.
>
> Because families are the first and, it is hoped, best faith builders of young people, our purpose is to provide activities that strengthen the bonds that already unite you as families and that build faith among you.

icebreaker: touch blue

Conduct this icebreaker by giving the following directions in your own words:

> As I ask you to touch something, quickly move about to touch it. If possible, move to a different person for each item. Several people may touch the same item at the same time. If you do not know a person you are about to touch, introduce yourself first. Ready? Move quickly.
> • Touch something blue.
> • Touch a watch.
> • Touch jeans.
> • Touch glasses.
> • Touch . . . [add other appropriate items]

16

icebreaker: round robin

Direct this icebreaker by giving the following directions in your own words:

> Please stand together as families. Now get into groups of eight families each [fewer if you have a small number of participants]. In your group, stand in parallel lines, with the adults in one line and the teens in the other line, facing the adults. Each teen should be standing directly across from an adult. If you have an uneven number, please raise your hand and we will adjust the groups. [Move people from group to group, if necessary.]
>
> You will have 1 minute to answer the questions or respond to the statements I will give you. Persons facing each other must answer or respond to each other. If you are standing across from a person whom you do not know, introduce yourself before answering the questions or statements. I will ring a bell [or make some other noise] to stop discussion of each question. In between each question or statement, I will call a halt and ask the teens to move one person to the right, with the teen on the end moving to the beginning of the line. Then, once each person has a new partner, I will continue with the next question or statement. Ready? Here is the first question:
>
> • What do you most like to do in your spare time?

After 1 minute, call a halt and ask the teens to move one person to the right. Continue this routine until you have covered the following questions:
> • Share one thing you like about school or your job.
> • If you were given one thousand dollars tomorrow, what would you do with it?
> • Name one person you really admire.
> • If you were given two hundred dollars but had to give half of it away, which charity would you give the one hundred dollars to?
> • If you could change one thing in our world, what would it be and why?
> • What do you like best about church?
> • [Add other appropriate questions or statements.]

Finally, ring the bell (or make some other noise) to end the icebreaker.

prayer

When you have completed the icebreakers, light the paschal candle that you have placed on a tall stand. Direct the group to divide into circles of four or five families each and stand close to one another. Address the groups in the following or similar words:

> Let us remember that we are in the presence of Jesus, the true light of the world. We have just spent time getting to know one another. We will now take time to pray for one another. I will light one candle for each circle from our paschal candle. One person from each group

should come and receive a lighted candle and then stand in her or his group and hold the candle. When the music begins, concentrate on the person who is holding the candle and thank God for the light she or he brings to our world. Pray silently for that person, that she or he may continue to reflect God's light in all that she or he does. Each of you will take turns holding the candle for about ten seconds and then silently passing it to the person on your left. All will pray for the person holding the candle. If your group finishes before the music ends, silently place the candle in the center of your circle and pray for all the members of your circle. If you have not finished when the music ends, continue until you have prayed for each person. Then place your candle on the floor in the center of your circle.

When the music stops and all the candles are in the center, say: Please join hands now within your circles and let us pray together a prayer of praise, the Glory Be:

> Glory be to the Father,
> and to the Son,
> and to the Holy Spirit.
> As it was in the beginning,
> is now, and ever shall be,
> world without end. Amen.

Make sure that someone in each circle blows out the candles.

special features of the experiences

Distribute a copy of handout 1–A, "Special Features of the Experiences," to each family and go over it with the participants, pointing out the special features of each faith experience.

Special Features of the Experiences

This event is full of activities. Each is designed to be experienced by one family at a time, except for "Highway to Heaven," for which two families will join together. The specific directions for each activity are on the table(s) where the activity is set up. This handout lists a few special features about each one. As you move from table to table, take it along as a reminder of these features. Please go through the activities slowly and thoughtfully, allowing everyone to express their viewpoints. After you have completed each experience, place a check mark in the circle next to its description below. Remember, we all have a piece of wisdom to share.

○ For the **"Say What"** activity, an easel is located in the center of the table(s). Attach your action statement, what you say, on the easel when you are finished. Be sure that you take a walk by the board later to see what others have said.

○ Enjoy the snacks at the table for **"Thanks for the Memories."** You will also find a treasure box in the middle of the table(s). This box is for you to put your thank-you note in, or you may choose to put your thank-you note in an envelope and mail it directly to the person you want to thank.

○ **"Highway to Heaven"** is a game two families play together. Be sure that each person gets to answer the questions fully. Listen carefully to one another. Wait for each person to respond before moving on.

○ Envelopes with cards in them are on the **"What's It to Ya?"** table(s). After looking at the sample collage, you each should take your own envelope and carefully put the cards in order. First you will put them in two piles: important and not important. Then you will put them in one vertical line, with the least important being on the bottom and the most important on the top. Place the cards carefully because you will have to explain your placement to your family. You can discover much about one another by knowing what you value least and most.

○ The **"Signed, Sealed, Delivered"** activity has two parts. In part A, look at the crosses. Pick them up and read their descriptions carefully. Are any of these types of crosses hanging in your home? For part B, read and follow the directions found on the table. This experience invites you to design a personal cross. Choose your colors carefully, noting that each color has a specific and special meaning.

After you have completed all the experiences, please fill out an evaluation sheet, found on the evaluation table. Your comments and ideas will assist us in planning future activities. There are separate evaluation sheets for teens and parents. After everyone has finished the evaluation, we will have a closing prayer. If your schedule permits, please stay for the prayer and refreshments. If not, feel free to depart. Have a wonderful time together. Enjoy the activities. We will be available if you have questions or need help.

Handout 1–A: Permission to reproduce this handout for program use is granted.

19

EXPERIENCE 2

say what?

focus

In both ordinary and extraordinary daily circumstances we are invited to live in friendship with God, walking in God's presence. "Say what?" explores the possibility of sin in ordinary situations, helping us recognize and, it is hoped, choose good over evil. We will then discover that making choices for good strengthens our relationship with God.

materials needed

You will need the following materials for this activity:
- ❍ a copy of resource 2–A, "Directions: Say What?" for each setting
- ❍ a 9-by-12-inch sheet of colored poster paper for each setting
- ❍ rubber cement or glue
- ❍ a laminator or clear contact paper
- ❍ two cut-out hearts for each setting (see resource 2–B, "Sin Is . . ." and resource 2–C, "God Says, I Say")
- ❍ a scissors
- ❍ crayons or markers
- ❍ an 8-inch piece of purple ribbon and an 8-inch piece of red ribbon for each setting
- ❍ a Bible for each setting
- ❍ a copy of handout 2–A, "Is It a Sin?" for each participant
- ❍ several copies of handout 2–B, "Cartoon Characters," cut apart, one set for each setting
- ❍ a basket to put the paper cartoon characters in, one for each setting
- ❍ a pencil or pen for each participant at each setting
- ❍ pins, glue, or tape at each setting to attach the action statements to the easel, bulletin board, or wall
- ❍ an easel with a felt pad, a bulletin board, or a wall to put the action statements on (If using an easel, have one at each setting.)
- ❍ a card labeled "Say What?" for each setting

preparation and setup

Prepare the materials and set up the experience as directed here for each setting you are using for this activity:
1. Make a copy of resource 2–A, "Directions: Say What?" Mount the copy on a sheet of colored poster paper. Laminate the poster paper or cover it with clear contact paper and place it on the table for this activity.
2. Copy, color, cut out, and laminate the heart on resource 2–B, "Sin Is. . . ." Take the 8-inch piece of *purple* ribbon and glue it to the back of the heart. Use this heart to mark 1 John 3:4 in a Bible and place it on the table.
3. Copy, color, cut out, and laminate the heart on resource 2–C, "God Says, I Say." Take the 8-inch piece of *red* ribbon and glue it to the back of the heart. Use this heart to mark Micah 6:8 in a Bible and place it on the table.
4. Make a copy of handout 2–A, "Is It a Sin?" for each participant. Place these on the table.
5. Copy and cut out a sufficient number and variety of cartoon characters from handout 2–B, "Cartoon Characters." Each participant will choose one from the basket.
6. Place on the table a card labeled "Say What?"

Directions:
Say What?

Is It a Sin?

- Each of you please take a copy of the handout titled "Is It a Sin?" Read situation 1 on the handout. What do you say—is it a sin or is it not a sin?
- On the handout, choose the thermometer that indicates your answer to situation 1 and fill it in to the degree that you are convinced of your choice (a high temperature means you are very convinced).
- Share your response to situation 1 with one another.
- Take turns explaining why you chose the answer you did.
- Respond to the other situations, using the same process.

God Says

- Open the Bible to the purple ribbon and read what the heart says sin is (1 John 3:4).
- Open the Bible to the red ribbon and read what "God says" (Micah 6:8). Discuss what sin is, what God says, and what you have to say about sin.

We Say

- Each of you take a cartoon character from the basket. Write on it one way that you will choose to live more closely to God. The "God Says" heart may be of help to you. Share your decision with one another. Post your cartoon character, with your action statement on it, on the board or other place provided for it.

Is It a Sin?

	Definitely! It's a sin!	No way! It's no sin!

1 What if I wanted to play a joke on my friend because she is always playing jokes on me? So I take a little soap bar (like the ones from a motel) and dip it in melted chocolate so that it is coated and looks just like a little candy bar. I wrap it in foil and give it to my friend. When my friend takes a bite and begins to chew, well, you can guess what happens!

What do you say—is it a sin?

2 John is so cool—he lives down the street and always has something to share with his friends, like candy or baseball cards, and sometimes even cigarettes! When he offered me some cigarettes, I asked him how he could afford to give away all these things. He said he doesn't pay for them, he just lifts them. What if I decide to accept his gifts anyway?

What do you say—is it a sin?

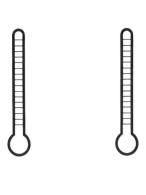

3 Sometimes fights break out in our school. You know, someone smarts off to a person or pushes another person around, and pretty soon they start fighting. It's usually during noon hour when there's really nothing else to do, so everyone usually gathers around and watches the action. What if I decide to join the circle and just watch?

What do you say—is it a sin?

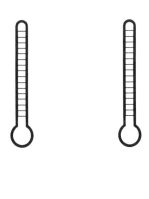

4 Sometimes we can't find anything to do at night, so we just go for a walk. And there's this big lot at the end of our street with just a storage shed on it. It makes a great target! Sometimes my friends throw rocks, balls, or whatever they can find at it—just to test their pitching arm, you know. What if I decide to test my arm, too?

What do you say—is it a sin?

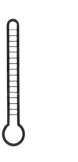

Handout 2–A: Permission to reproduce this handout for program use is granted.

23

Sin Is . . .

Everyone who commits sin is guilty of lawlessness; sin is lawlessness (1 John 3:4).

Discuss.

Sin Is . . .
- choosing to turn away from God
- choosing to hurt others or ourselves
- refusing to do what we know is right
- knowing something is wrong but choosing to do it anyway

Attach purple ribbon.

Resource 2–B: Permission to reproduce this resource for program use is granted.

God Says, I Say

God Says . . .

- Do what is right and just,
- love tenderly,
- walk humbly with me.
  (Adapted from Micah 6:8)

I Say . . .

- choose to live honestly
- choose to get involved
- choose to accept the consequences of my actions
- choose to respect other people and their property

Discuss.

Attach red ribbon.

Cartoon Characters

Handout 2–B: Permission to reproduce this handout for program use is granted.

Cartoon Characters *(continued)*

27

Jump forward two spaces

HIGHWAY

Jump forward three spaces

Jump forward three spaces

K **TO** **HEAVEN**

ven

Jump back
three
spaces

Jump
back
two spaces

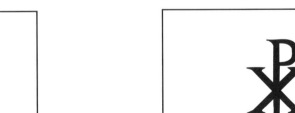

START

EXPERIENCE 3

thanks for the memories

focus

Remembering times, events, and persons can help us see relationships in a new light and grow in gratitude for them and the wisdom gained from them. Experience 3 activates the memory to help us appreciate our relationships with family, friends, and God.

materials needed

You will need the following materials for this activity:

❍ a copy of resource 3–A, "Directions: Thanks for the Memories," for each setting
❍ a 9-by-12-inch sheet of colored poster paper for each setting
❍ rubber cement or glue
❍ a laminator or clear contact paper
❍ a copy of handout 3–A, "Our Family Tree," for each family
❍ a memory card on colored paper for each person (see handout 3–B, "Memory Cards")
❍ a scissors
❍ a pen or pencil for each participant at each setting
❍ a treasure box for the memory cards at each setting
❍ a container to hold the memory cards at each setting
❍ envelopes for memory cards (to be available at each setting for mailing purposes)
❍ a bowl of snacks at each setting
❍ a card labeled "Thanks for the Memories," for each setting

preparation and setup

Prepare the materials and set up for the experience as directed here for each setting you are using for this activity:

1. Make a copy of resource 3–A, "Directions: Thanks for the Memories." Mount the copy on a sheet of colored poster paper. Laminate the poster paper or cover it with clear contact paper and place it on the table designated for this experience.
2. Make a copy of handout 3–A, "Our Family Tree," for each family. Place the copies on the table.
3. Make one copy of handout 3–B, "Memory Cards," for every four participants. Make the copies on colored paper; one card is needed for each person. Cut the cards apart, fold each one in half horizontally so that "Dear God" appears on the front, and place them in a container on the table.
4. Construct or bring a treasure box for the memory cards. Have envelopes available on the table for those who prefer to mail their memory card.
5. Prepare a bowl of snacks for this setting. Be ready to refill the bowl.
6. Place on the table a card labeled "Thanks for the Memories."

Directions:
Thanks for the Memories

1. Pick up a copy of the handout "Our Family Tree." Together, fill in the names of your immediate family in the branches of the tree.

2. Take turns sharing a favorite memory you have about one of your family members. Explain why you still hold this memory. Share other favorite family memories.

3. Together, jot down favorite family memories on the family tree roots.

4. Reflect on the following aspects of memories:
   - Memories play an important part in our relationships with family, friends, and God.
   - Without memories, we would repeat our past mistakes and feel lost and alone.
   - Without memories, we would not be able to learn from one another or have the pleasure of remembering our family members and the good times we have shared.
   - Without memories, we would not have "roots" in the past to anchor us for our journey into the future.

5. Share how a memory has helped guide you, such as, Through a car accident I learned that _____ and so now I _____ _____. Or, through my anger I learned that blowing up hurts others, so now I _____.

6. Share a memory of how the church or God has been a part of your family.

7. Take a memory card. Inside the card, write a thank-you to someone for a good memory. For example, write to Grandma and thank her for always having chocolate-chip cookies when you come to visit.

8. Put the memory card in the treasure box, or put it inside an envelope and mail it to the person whom you are thanking.

Our Family Tree

Memory Cards

Handout 3–B: Permission to reproduce this handout for program use is granted.

EXPERIENCE 4

highway to heaven

focus

"Highway to heaven" focuses on eternal union with God as the final destination of our Christian journey. Called through baptism to grow as persons, we come to know God by understanding and living our faith in community.

materials needed

You will need the following materials for this activity:
- ○ a copy of the game board from resource 4–A, "Highway to Heaven," for each setting
- ○ pink, blue, yellow, green, and red markers or crayons
- ○ two 11-by-17-inch sheets of colored poster paper
- ○ three 9-by-12-inch sheets for each setting: one yellow, one green, one blue
- ○ rubber cement or glue
- ○ a laminator or clear contact paper
- ○ a double-sided copy of resources 4–B, "Card Set 1," 4–C, "Card Set 2," and 4–D, "Card Set 3" for each setting
- ○ a scissors
- ○ a game token for each player (e.g., buttons as tokens)
- ○ a copy of resource 4–E, "Directions: Highway to Heaven," for each setting
- ○ a die for each setting
- ○ a card labeled "Highway to Heaven," for each setting

preparation and setup

Prepare the materials and set up for the experience as directed here for each setting you are using for this activity:
1. Photocopy the game board found in the center spread of this book, and color in the boxes on it according to the following specifications:
   - Use pink for boxes with directions.
   - Use green for boxes with the flower symbol.
   - Use blue for boxes with the people symbol.
   - Use yellow for boxes with the Chi-Rho symbol.
   - Use red for the arrows on the board.
   - Color the area marked "heaven" any color.
2. After coloring in the boxes, mount the game board on brightly colored poster paper, laminate it, or cover it with clear contact paper.
3. Photocopy the game cards from resources 4–B, 4–C, and 4–D onto colored poster paper. Use yellow paper for card set 1, green paper for card set 2, and blue paper for card set 3. Make sure the symbol for each set is photocopied onto the backs of the cards. Cut the cards apart and place them in their respective boxes on the game board.
4. Make a copy of resource 4–E, "Directions: Highway to Heaven," mount it on poster paper, and laminate it. Place the directions in a standing position (if possible) on the table.
5. Set up only one "Highway to Heaven" experience at each table. Because two families will be participating at the same time, set up six chairs (more if some families have more than one child attending).
6. Place on the table a card labeled "Highway to Heaven."

36

Card Set 1

Card Set 1 *(continued)*

Why do you think God gave us the Ten Commandments?	Describe Jesus.	Name a commandment that is a challenge to live and explain why.
Name items in your home that let others know that you are a Catholic.	God is like . . .	Name a favorite prayer and explain why you like it.
What do you think heaven will be like?	The Holy Spirit is like . . .	Why was Jesus put to death?
What do you like about being a Catholic?	Name our pope and the bishop of our diocese.	Why is Easter the church's biggest feast?
What do you find hard about being a Catholic?	Name one special thing about your parish.	Name items in your home that let others know that you are a Catholic.
How do you like to pray?	Name a church season and tell why it is special to you.	What is special about Mary?
What is the Bible?	Name the sacraments you have received.	When do you like to pray?

Card Set 2

Card Set 2 *(continued)*

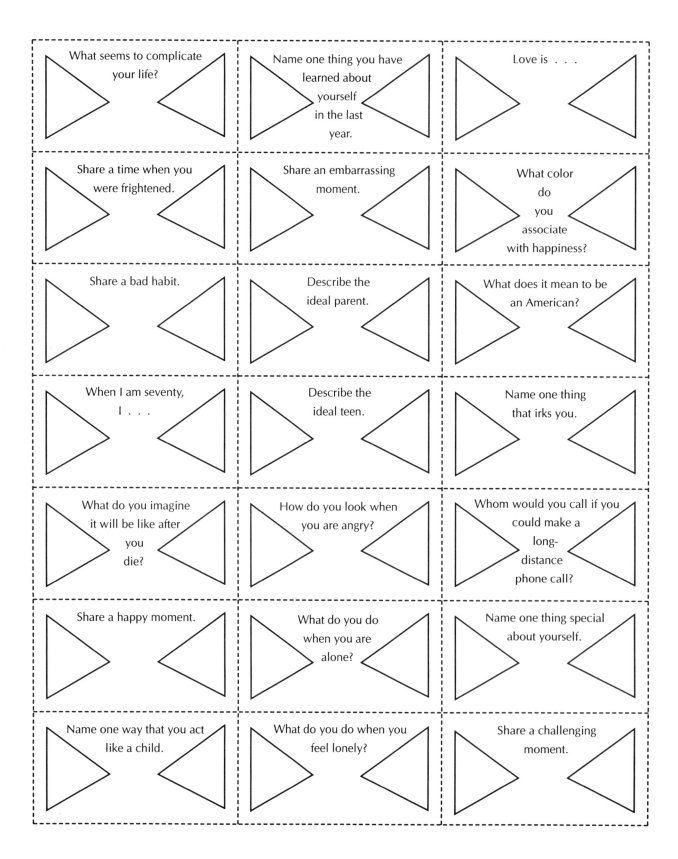

What seems to complicate your life?

Name one thing you have learned about yourself in the last year.

Love is . . .

Share a time when you were frightened.

Share an embarrassing moment.

What color do you associate with happiness?

Share a bad habit.

Describe the ideal parent.

What does it mean to be an American?

When I am seventy, I . . .

Describe the ideal teen.

Name one thing that irks you.

What do you imagine it will be like after you die?

How do you look when you are angry?

Whom would you call if you could make a long-distance phone call?

Share a happy moment.

What do you do when you are alone?

Name one thing special about yourself.

Name one way that you act like a child.

What do you do when you feel lonely?

Share a challenging moment.

Card Set 3

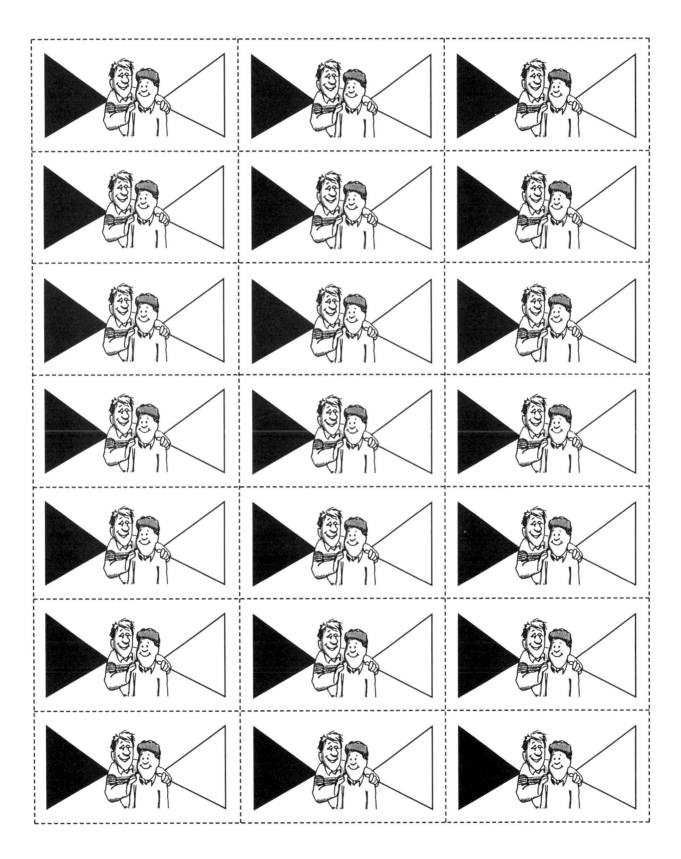

Card Set 3 *(continued)*

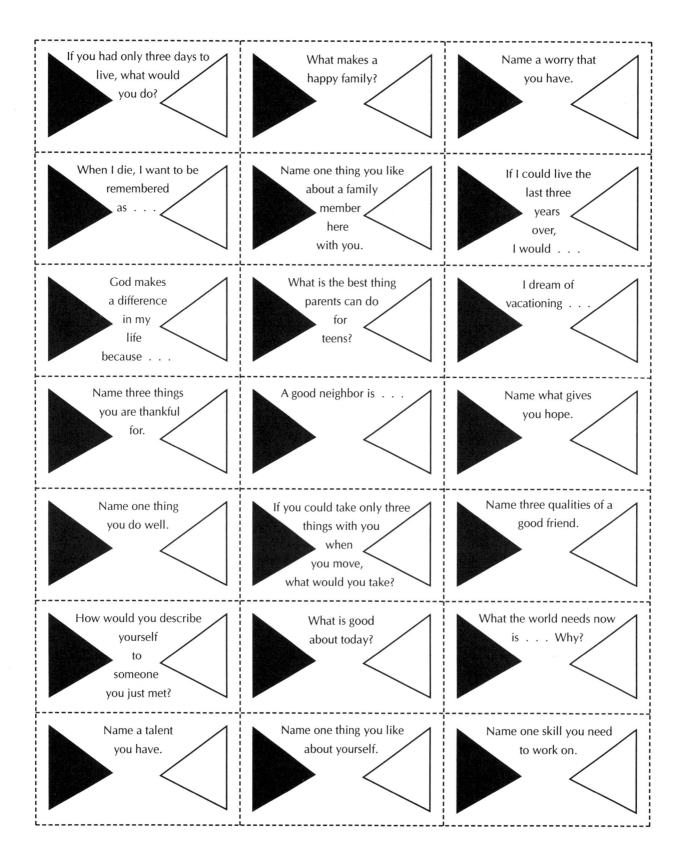

If you had only three days to live, what would you do?

What makes a happy family?

Name a worry that you have.

When I die, I want to be remembered as . . .

Name one thing you like about a family member here with you.

If I could live the last three years over, I would . . .

God makes a difference in my life because . . .

What is the best thing parents can do for teens?

I dream of vacationing . . .

Name three things you are thankful for.

A good neighbor is . . .

Name what gives you hope.

Name one thing you do well.

If you could take only three things with you when you move, what would you take?

Name three qualities of a good friend.

How would you describe yourself to someone you just met?

What is good about today?

What the world needs now is . . . Why?

Name a talent you have.

Name one thing you like about yourself.

Name one skill you need to work on.

Directions:
Highway to Heaven

Lake Van

Sin the moongod, honoured
particularly by the Aramaeans

Carchemish   Haran

Nabu, the god of the art of writi
(as well as other gods)

Dur Sharrukin
Nineveh

Aleppo
d, the weathergod

Ishtar, goddess of love and war

Ebla
Dagan, the lord of the country

Ashur the na
of the

Hamath
Baal-Shamai

**Are you ready to start
Highway to Heaven?**

- Place your tokens on the start. Each
  player rolls the die once. The person
  with the highest roll starts.
- Roll the die and move your token accord-
  ingly. Heaven is your destination. If you
  land on the character squares, draw
  the corresponding card and share your
  answer with the others. Invite them to
  respond to you.

The journey ends when the first player reaches
heaven with an exact roll. Have fun!

  After finishing the game, share one
thing you learned from this journey.
Then move to the next open table.

Damascus
Hadad Ramma
thunderer, and h

ea of Chinnereth
(Sea of Galilee)

Rabbath-ammon
AMMON   Milkom,
         the national god of the Ammonites

Yhwh is the god of the whole earth, the mountains of Judah belong to him,
the God of Jerusalem' (inscription from Khirbet Beth-lei, about 700 bc)

MOAB
Kir-moab
Chemosh, the national god of the Moabites

EDOM
Edom, the territory of the god Qaus,
later Qos (a weathergod?), the national god of the Edomites

EXPERIENCE
5

signed, sealed, delivered

focus

We explore the meaning of the cross in this experience. The cross is rich in symbolism; it expresses our belief in the death and Resurrection of Jesus and our hope and trust that God will be present at each step of our life journey.

materials needed

You will need the following materials for this activity:

for part A

○ a tablecloth for each setting
○ a copy of part A of resource 5–A, "Directions: Signed, Sealed, Delivered, I'm Yours," for each setting
○ rubber cement or glue
○ one 9-by-12-inch sheet and one 11-by-17-inch sheet of colored poster paper for each setting
○ a laminator or clear contact paper
○ four crosses for each setting (The first three crosses listed below can be obtained from a local Catholic bookstore or from Autom, 5226 South Thirty-first Street, Phoenix, AZ 85040; phone 800-521-2914. The El Salvador cross can be obtained from Tree of Life Imports, 6941 Calumet Avenue, Hammond, IN 46324; phone 800-366-8654.)
   • Christ crucified cross
   • Resurrection cross
   • San Damiano cross
   • El Salvador cross
○ a copy of resource 5–B, "Descriptions of Crosses," for each setting
○ a scissors
○ a card labeled "Signed, Sealed, Delivered, I'm Yours: Part A," for each setting

for part B

○ a copy of part B of resource 5–A, "Directions: Signed, Sealed, Delivered, I'm Yours," for each setting
○ rubber cement or glue
○ a 9-by-12-inch sheet of colored poster paper for each setting
○ a laminator or clear contact paper
○ a copy of handout 5–A, "Sealed," for each participant
○ colored beads for each participant (refer to handout 5–A for the twelve colors that are needed; each person chooses five beads)
○ a 30-inch piece of leather cord for each participant
○ a sample of a beaded cross for each setting
○ a card labeled "Signed, Sealed, Delivered, I'm Yours: Part B," for each setting

preparation and setup

Prepare the following materials and set up for the experience as directed here for each setting you are using for this activity:

for part A

1. Cover the table with a cloth.
2. Photocopy part A of resource 5–A, "Directions: Signed, Sealed, Delivered, I'm Yours," mount it on a 9-by-12-inch sheet of colored poster paper and fold it so that it will stand up, and laminate it or cover it with clear contact paper and place it on the table and label them.
3. Place the four crosses on the table and label each one.
4. Photocopy resource 5–B, "Descriptions of Crosses," and mount it on an 11-by-17-inch sheet of colored poster paper so that it can be folded to stand up.
5. Place the descriptions with the crosses.
6. Place on the table a card labeled "Signed, Sealed, Delivered, I'm Yours: Part A."

for part B

1. Photocopy part B of resource 5–A, "Directions: Signed, Sealed, Delivered, I'm Yours," mount it on colored poster paper and fold it so that it will stand up, and laminate it or cover it with clear contact paper and place it on the table.
2. Make a copy of handout 5–A, "Sealed," for each participant.
3. Place a sufficient number and variety of colored beads on the table. (See handout 5–A for the list of colors needed.)
4. Place the leather cords on the table, one for each participant.
5. Place a sample of a beaded cross on the table. (Refer to part B of resource 5–A for an illustration of a beaded cross.)
6. Place on the table a card labeled "Signed, Sealed, Delivered, I'm Yours: Part B."

Signed, Sealed, Delivered, I'm Yours

Directions for "Signed, Sealed, Delivered: Part A"

Pick up the crosses on the table. Look at them. Read the description of each cross. Then discuss these questions:
- Have you seen any of these crosses in churches? in homes?
- Which cross is your favorite? Discuss.

Now move on to part B.

Directions for "Signed, Sealed, Delivered: Part B"

Signed

Each participant silently reads the following reflection on the meaning of the cross:

> As Catholics, the cross is our symbol of belief in Jesus, who lived, suffered, died, was buried, and rose again from the dead for us so that we, too, might have everlasting life. The cross is our symbol of hope and faith in our one true God. The cross reminds us that even though we may have problems, pain, and suffering in our life, our trust in God will always bring us joy.
>
> At our baptism, we were marked with the sign of the cross. Our parents and godparents said yes for us, indicating that we agreed to follow Jesus. Each day we are challenged to follow Jesus wholeheartedly.
>
> As a reminder of the cross we were sealed with in baptism, we will make our own personal cross. Following Jesus brings challenges, joys, and pain, but new life as well. Your cross will be made up of colors that represent the challenges, pain, and new life that following Jesus brings to you.

Sealed

Pick up a copy of handout 5–A, "Sealed," which explains the symbolism of each bead color. Then make your own personal cross by following these directions:
1. Take a leather cord.
2. Select five beads in the colors that symbolize the characteristics you need in order to follow Jesus more closely.
3. Make the cross as illustrated in the diagram. Begin with the bead in the center.
4. Pull the cord tight at the end of each step.
5. After all of you have finished making your cross, share with one another the meaning of your cross. Explain the reasons behind each bead color you chose. How does your cross indicate the ways that you will follow Jesus?

Delivered, I'm Yours

1. Put your cross around your neck.
2. As you put your cross on, say together, "Yes, I will follow Jesus."
3. Wear your cross as a symbol of your decision to walk more closely to Jesus.

Signed, Sealed, Delivered, I'm Yours

Directions for "Signed, Sealed, Delivered: Part A"

Pick up the crosses on the table. Look at them. Read the description of each cross. Then discuss these questions:
- Have you seen any of these crosses in churches? in homes?
- Which cross is your favorite? Discuss.

Now move on to part B.

Directions for "Signed, Sealed, Delivered: Part B"

Signed

Each participant silently reads the following reflection on the meaning of the c

> As Catholics, the cross is our symbol of belief in Jesus, who lived, suffer
> died, was buried, and rose again from the dead for us so that we, too, migl
> have everlasting life. The cross is our symbol of hope and faith in our one
> God. The cross reminds us that even though we may have problems, pain,
> and suffering in our life, our trust in God will always bring us joy.
>
> At our baptism, we were marked with the sign of the cross. Our
> parents and godparents said yes for us, indicating that we agreed to
> follow Jesus. Each day we are challenged to follow Jesus wholeheartedly.
>
> As a reminder of the cross we were sealed with in baptism, we will mal
> our own personal cross. Following Jesus brings challenges, joys, and pain,
> new life as well. Your cross will be made up of colors that represent the ch
> lenges, pain, and new life that following Jesus brings to you.

Sealed

Pick up a copy of handout 5–A, "Sealed," which explains the symbolism of ea
bead color. Then make your own personal cross by following these directions:
1. Take a leather cord.
2. Select five beads in the colors that symbolize the characteristics you need in order to follow Jesus more closely.
3. Make the cross as illustrated in the diagram. Begin with the bead in the center.
4. Pull the cord tight at the end of each step.
5. After all of you have finished making your cross, share with one another the meaning of your cross. Explain the reasons behind each bead color you chose. How does your cross indicate the ways that you will follow Jesus?

Delivered, I'm Yours
1. Put your cross around your neck.
2. As you put your cross on, say together, "Yes, I will follow Jesus."
3. Wear your cross as a symbol of your decision to walk more closely to Jesus.

Descriptions of Crosses

Resurrection Cross

This cross celebrates the new life won for all of us because of Jesus' suffering, death, and Resurrection. It reminds us that death and sin have no power over Jesus, and that one day we, too, will rise to be with Jesus forever if we follow his ways.

El Salvador Cross

Many of the people of El Salvador live in extreme poverty, but they are spiritually very rich. They see their God as the one who makes all life possible— their spirits, the earth, their animals, and their crops.

Christ Crucified Cross

Jesus was crucified for the sins of all people. He challenged the people of his day to turn from their selfish ways, and they put him to death. Through the suffering and death of Jesus, our sins are forgiven and we have the chance to live forever with him in eternity.

San Damiano Cross

Saint Francis was said to be praying before a crucifix like this in the church of San Damiano when the figure of Jesus spoke to him from the cross. "Francis," the voice said, "go and rebuild my church." Soon after this, Saint Francis began to preach the Gospel and bring peace to troubled people. Many men and women became his followers, and today the Franciscans, as they are called, are preaching the word of God all over the world. This cross, like the one in the church where Francis heard Jesus speak, is called the San Damiano cross.

Sealed

Look at and think about the symbolism of the different colors listed below. Each color represents a special characteristic that Jesus lived and modeled for others. Note which characteristics you especially need to adopt in order to continue to follow Jesus.

Orange Strength to stand in the "fire" of troubled relationships with family and friends

White Hope in the promise of everlasting life with Jesus

Tan Respect for ourselves and the earth—we are made from the earth and in the image and likeness of God

Yellow God's light to light our way and lead us out of darkness

Black The absence of all color—for equality between all people, regardless of their skin color or beliefs

Green Growth—the Holy Spirit helps us grow in body, mind, and spirit

Red Courage to stand up for and speak out about what we believe

Pink The color of the dawn—for trust in a new day, a new beginning with God

Turquoise Ourselves as precious gems in God's eyes

Gray Ashes, for letting go of our past failures and mistakes

Blue God's refreshing waters that wash away all our sins

Purple Patience in suffering the trials of our daily life

Now make your personal cross by following the instructions given on the directions sheet.

EXPERIENCE 6

what's it to ya?

focus

"What's it to ya?" explores how people's values change and grow over time. For example, things that were once very important to us may seem insignificant to us now. Our words and actions often reveal the values we presently hold. In this activity, we discover and share the important value of God and church in our life.

materials needed

You will need the following materials for this activity:

- ○ a sample collage for each setting, depicting various values, for example, friends, clothes, sports (see resource 6–A, "Sample Collage")
- ○ a copy of resource 6–B, "Directions: What's It to Ya?" for each setting
- ○ a 9-by-12-inch sheet of colored poster paper for each setting
- ○ rubber cement or glue
- ○ a laminator or clear contact paper
- ○ three copies of resource 6–C, "Value Cards" for each setting (more copies are needed if you have family groups of more than three people)
- ○ three envelopes for each setting (more envelopes are needed if you have family groups of more than three people)
- ○ a scissors
- ○ a pen or pencil
- ○ a card labeled "What's It to Ya?" for each setting

preparation and setup

Prepare the following materials and set up for the experience as directed here for each setting you are using for this activity:

1. Create a collage that highlights values embraced by teens and adults. (See resource 6–A, "Sample Collage.")
2. Photocopy resource 6–B, "Directions: What's It to Ya?" Mount the copy on a piece of colored poster paper. Laminate the poster paper or cover it with clear contact paper and place it on the table designated for this activity.
3. Make three (or more) copies of resource 6–C, "Value Cards." Cut each set of cards apart and place each set in a different envelope. Mark the front of each envelope with the title of this activity, "What's It To Ya?"
4. Place the envelopes on the table.
5. Place on the table a card labeled "What's It to Ya?"

Sample Collage

Resource 6–A: Permission to reproduce this resource for program use is granted.

Directions:
What's It to Ya?

11

1. Look at the sample collage. Share with one another images in the collage that are important to you. For example, friends, clothes, television, sports, money, music.

2. Each of you take an envelope of value cards. Spread the cards out before you. Look at the cards. Which of these items is important in your life? Which have not been that important in your life? Sort the cards into two piles: one pile for your important values and the other pile for values that have not been that important to you.

3. In silence, rank your "not important" cards, putting the least important card on the bottom. Take the "important" cards and rank them the same way, placing the most important card on the top. Now lay out all your cards in a vertical line, with the most important card at the top and the least important card at the bottom.

4. Share your bottom card (least important). Why is this value not important to you?

5. Share your top card (most important). Why is this value so important to you?

6. Explain why you placed the other cards as you did.

7. Name one thing that you learned about one another from this activity.

8. Discuss values as . . .
   • what we consider to be most important to us
   • what we are willing to sacrifice for
   • treasures we live by
   • being different for everyone

9. Parent(s), share how these values have changed for you since you were a teen.

10. Teen(s), share how these values have changed for you in the last year or two.

11. Show one another, if you haven't already done so, where you placed God and the church in your ranking of values. Explain why you placed those cards where you did.

12. Put the cards back in the envelopes and move on to another experience.

Value Cards

Family	Church
Friends	What Others Think
Television	Sports
School or Work	Teachers or Employers
Money	God
Music	Clothes

Endorsements continued from back cover:

"I enjoyed sharing values with my mom. We were both surprised when we picked the same colors for our necklaces. I learned a lot about myself and my mom through these experiences." **Elizabeth Sturm,** grade 8, Saint Bernard's Parish, Stewartville, Minnesota

"When asked to evaluate the experiences, parents and teens consistently give two responses: They like *most* being together and discovering more about each other, and they wish this kind of experience could take place more often. For my part, I see offering parents and children tools by which they can deepen their relationship with God and each other as primary in the role of a faith community and in my role as a religious educator." **Marybeth Sands,** director of religious education, Saint Mary's Parish, Winona, Minnesota